How to Live with A Narcissist Husband

A Comprehensive Guide to Understanding, Dealing with, and Recovering from Narcissistic Abuse

Scout Simon

Table of contents

Induction

Narcissism can make it hard for people to get along in relationships. Some people talk about how difficult their life is with a narcissistic husband or wife. They may say things like cheating, being selfish, or being difficult to deal with.

There are a few things you can do to cope with a husband who is narcissistic. First, remember that you don't have to do everything he wants. You also have the right to set boundaries and have your own life. And finally, don't hesitate to talk to a friend or family member for help if you feel like you're struggling.

A narcissist is like a bucket with a hole in the bottom. He or she can never be satisfied with how much they have, so no matter how much you give them, they'll always want more.

Narcissism is a personality disorder that is focused on oneself. People with this disorder have an inflated sense of their own worth, and often struggle to get along with others. This can make life very difficult for them, especially in relationships.

If you're noticing signs that your partner may be narcissistic, that's not necessarily a bad thing. In fact, it can help you to understand them better. However, it's important to remember that narcissistic behavior is not always easy to deal with. But we can help you to cope with it.

Chapter 1

Understanding who is a narcissistic Husband

If you are married to a person who is very narcissistic, they may do things to you that will destroy your life. If you are starting to think that you may be married to someone like this, congratulations! It can be hard to spot when you are being controlled, so you should thank yourself for your bravery.

The first step is being able to identify the reality of your situation. Then, you have to deal with it by getting away from the abuser, and undoing any damage he's done.

The more information you have about what your husband did and how he did it, the better off you will be. This is because he may have created a "false personality" to control and manipulate you. This false personality can be different from the real you in many ways, and understanding it will help you to protect yourself.

If you have a partner who always puts their own needs first, and insists on controlling everything, that's called psychological abuse. It's like if your boss always made you work late, or if your best friend always pushed her own agenda onto you.

When you eat something, the food goes into your stomach and then your intestines. Your intestines are like a tube that takes the food all the way down to your feet. There, your body can use the food to make energy.

A narcissistic husband is someone who is very focused on having control over you. He wants all of your time and attention, and he wants you to think of him as the most important thing in your life. He will manipulate your beliefs, control your thinking and your decision making, and manage your behaviors. He will even change how you think about the world and your place in it.

The changes you're noticing in yourself – like friends saying you're different, not yourself, and not knowing who you are – are all due to a change in your personality, caused by your husband. He has been using a fake personality to control you.

The effects of narcissistic abuse can be long-term, and the person may never be able to rid themselves of the pseudo-personality. If you are in a relationship with someone who has a narcissistic personality, it is important to be aware of the signs so you can help them cope and heal. This type of personality is made up of different parts that are designed to make the person look good in the eyes of the abuser. It can make them feel strong and in control, even when they are really feeling weak and powerless.

We'll talk about the pseudo-personality in more detail in this article. It's a kind of personality that doesn't really exist in reality, and it can have some important implications.

Some things are made out of different materials, like wood and plastic. Some materials can't be cut or torn, like metal.

Deception from day one

From the very first encounter, the narcissist plays with the impressions of the victims. They are charming, friendly, and caring, as well as intelligent, wise, and worldly, the narcissist explains. They understand that first impressions are important and they want to make the best they can be. My grandfather used to say, "Get an early riser name and you can stay in bed all day!"

Narcissists want people to look up to them because that gives them a power imbalance in the relationship. They use this power to get what they want (praise, compliments, and adoration) from those around them.

The narcissistic husband uses a range of mind control techniques to change the way the wife thinks, feels, and behaves. This changes her personality in a way that is not always comfortable or desirable.

I have a friend who is really good at math. He can do math problems really quickly.

The pseudo-personality is a kind of personality that contains the programming and beliefs that the narcissistic husband wants in place. This personality behaves and thinks like the narcissist, with the goal of making the narcissist's life more comfortable.

In a situation like this, one person (the slave) does not realize that they are being controlled and treated like a slave. They believe that they are making their own choices and that the relationship is normal. The slave thinks that others in the situation are also working hard for the benefit of all.

Sometimes people do things that seem strange or impossible, like making someone do something they don't want to do. This is sometimes called mind control.

The personality that is programmed to care about the happiness of the narcissistic husband is usually very careful not to do anything that could make him upset. This includes making decisions that may not be in the best interest of the person, because we want to avoid causing him any pain. We often do things without really thinking about it, because we've become used to thinking that it's the best way to please him.

A pseudo-personality is like a pretend personality. It's made up, and it believes it is making its own decisions. However, the pseudo-personality is really just following the decisions that have been made about it up to that point. The pseudo-personality doesn't have a choice in the matter, and it doesn't understand the extensive influence the narcissist has had on it. The pseudo-personality is motivated to stay in the relationship and try to improve things because it believes it is doing things on its own.

Dependency

The pseudo-personality is conditioned to be very dependent on the narcissistic partner.

This begins out with the woman requiring to verify with him to know what to do. If often ends up with her needing to verify with him to know if she is ok and even to know who she is.

The notion is that she feels that if he is ok, then she is ok, too. If he is furious or disturbed, then she feels terrible and she may even consider that she is bad. She has been physically conditioned to assume accountability for anything that goes wrong, and if he is unhappy, then she is at blame, and it's because of who she is that there are difficulties. This kind of reasoning is very deleterious to a person's self-respect and self-confidence. It implies that the pseudo-personality often has a very poor estimation of itself.

But to strangers, the pseudo personality projects a fantastic façade. It behaves as if everything is wonderful and the relationship is magnificent. In instances like this, when the woman separates from the narcissistic husband, people are surprised because they believe the two form the 'perfect pairing' and there did not seem to be an indication of any problems at all. They often find it hard to believe the long-suffering wife's accounts of her violent husband.

The pseudo personality is also conditioned to protect the narcissistic partner, making justifications for him when others criticize him. Even when the woman's relatives can see that he is violent, she backs him up. This can be very distressing for her family because they can't comprehend how she cannot see that he is evil and violent.

The interdependence can be such that a woman cannot envision a future without her narcissistic partner. Many people are anxious about fleeing and even believe they would be so alone that they could even perish. This undoubtedly leaves them trapped in the relationship with no other choice than to remain and try and make things work in whatever manner they can.

Responsibility

Having a pseudo-personality implies that a person's judgments and behaviors are not their own. These things have been molded and influenced by the narcissistic partner using an influence that is outside the consciousness of the sufferer.

The sufferer does not realize what is going on. They do not have all the information about their predicament. Not having complete knowledge and understanding of what is going on means that the woman's judgments are not fully informed.

She is making judgments with only a percentage of the accessible information, and even much of that is distorted! For this reason, the sufferer is not accountable for what occurred to them. (This typically takes a person month of study to fully understand how and why this is true.)

Things a violent partner says

Two Personalities

The pseudo-personality co-exists with the actual personality but it dominates and diminishes it. This concept helps to explain the emotional struggle that many women experience while with a narcissistic partner.

One portion of them desires one thing. Another portion desires the contrary.

The true disposition wishes to abandon the relationship. The pseudo-personality is programmed to remain. The pseudo-personality can hardly wait for him to return to the house, the real personality is horrified at the thought of being with him again. The pseudo-personality adores him, the true personality dislikes the things he does. The pseudo-personality feels that it needs to look after him, the actual personality rationally understands the circumstance is not equitable, terrible, or even deleterious.

These contradicting feelings, or contradictory thoughts and emotions, are very distressing for the woman and there is no way to rectify this situation until the pseudo-personality is eliminated.

While it is in place, however, the woman, not comprehending what is being done to her, can easily fault herself for not being able to work things out. Many ladies believe that they may be getting insane! And at the same time, they also have a feeling that it's not them that is the problem but that there is something wrong with them, but they just can't place their finger on what it is.

Durability

A narcissistic partner establishes a pseudo-personality over time using powerful influence techniques that are performed time and time again. The pseudo-personality is pushed onto the subject without their awareness or permission.

The target is therefore not in a position to oppose psychologically. In reality, in the honeymoon period of the relationship, the sufferer is a 'voluntary' collaborator, so to speak. This is the essence of mind control; the target believes that the offender is actually assisting them and is sincerely watching out for them. Therefore, it is simple for them to go along with what is occurring.

You can learn more about how pseudo-personality makes it hard to identify the symptoms of a domineering relationship.

These variables, along with the reality that a person's fundamental beliefs are altered, imply that the pseudo-personality can be quite enduring. Just because a woman departs a narcissistic partner does not mean that the pseudo-personality dissipates. It actually continues and it will last for decades unless the sufferer does something about it.

Some elements of the pseudo-personality may dissipate or diminish with time, but most of it does not.

First of all, the continuation of the belief system and behavior patterns, which are not intended for the benefit of the sufferer, creates problems of all kinds with confidence, relationships, sleep, concentration, memory, decision-making, intestinal issues, identity issues, and emotional difficulties.

Secondly, if a person does not acknowledge that they were in a violent relationship, they split up and try and put things behind them. Later, when problems occur, they do not correlate these problems with the violent relationship and the pseudo-personality.

They may seek assistance for said difficulties without understanding where the problems originated. Unless the psychiatrist identifies the foundation of the problem as being the violent relationship, the problem will be addressed in seclusion. This rarely provides satisfactory outcomes.

More violent circumstances

An individual who has a pseudo-personality has different beliefs, attitudes, and behaviors that have been implanted as part of the pseudo-personality. Pseudo-personalities share many similar beliefs and behaviors because each pseudo-personality is intended to be subordinate, submissive, dependent, and faithful.

For example, the pseudo-personality is conditioned to assume accountability whenever things go wrong so that many people fault themselves when anything around them is not working out.

They do this even when there is no possibility that circumstances are their responsibility. The behavioral representation of this pattern is the pseudo-personality of apologizing very frequently, even for the slightest of things.

Another frequent characteristic of pseudo-personality is demonstrated when somebody treats a pseudo-personality very kindly.

The pseudo-personality is so used to being treated poorly that when someone treats it well, it is extremely thankful. So thankful that it wants to make sure that the person doing the pleasant things knows how grateful it is.

What do you notice? The pseudo personality says 'thank you' a lot and may be very excessive in demonstrating appreciation, including going over the top in returning the good behavior, purchasing a small present, and so on.

The excessive apologizing and professing of appreciation are but two instances of evidence of the existence of a pseudo-personality. All kinds of other attitudes and behaviors indicate that a person has been manipulated or mistreated in the past if you know what you are looking for.

Psychopaths and narcissists know precisely what they are searching for. They recognize these indicators as soon as they encounter someone. After all, they are used to inflicting these things on their captives!

The reason this is essential is that when a psychopath, sociopath, or narcissist encounters a new individual if they see the indications of a pseudo-personality, they know that person will be an easy target for them. So they put their crosshairs on them and go for it.

This is why many people wind up in one violent circumstance after another, in one group after another, or have one narcissistic partner after another. People do not attract narcissists and psychopaths. These kinds are offenders and they are attracted to individuals who have already been mistreated.

The only way to remove the bullseye off your back is to get away from your pseudo-personality. Trying to ignore your violent circumstances will never work. The injury is too profound and you can't conceal it from the predators. You don't even know what they are searching for, so how can you conceal from them?!

Trying to control narcissists and psychopaths won't work either. They are so much more cunning and deceptive than you could ever be, and they are way better at dismantling bounds and boundaries than you ever will be at setting them in place.

A further complication here is that the pseudo-personality is programmed to disclose information about itself. The narcissistic husband needs information to keep the manipulation continuing so he programs the pseudo-personality to disclose things to him.

This pattern is pernicious and often extremely powerful and when a woman departs her narcissistic partner, the pattern continues. She ends up divulging all kinds of details about herself to others, often strangers.

If the observer or viewer is a narcissist, the woman is providing them with all the data they need to take up where the narcissistic partner left off.

So, what to do about a narcissistic partner

You need to depart. While you are in the relationship, the abuse continues, the pseudo-personality is continually reaffirmed and you struggle while your life is being snatched away from you. I realize it's exceedingly challenging to get out and it's still something that has to be done.

Then you have to remove the pseudo-personality. Working with a professional is worth your while. It will save you time, money, and heartache. Having professional assistance going through a divorce from someone you know is violent, and who is guaranteed to play dishonestly, is invaluable.

Until you get clear of the pseudo-personality you will have that guy in your mind, functioning like a malevolent psychotherapist. Your existence won't be your own and you will continue to be influenced by him.

If there are children, you owe it to them to get rid of your pseudo-personality so that you can assist them to get rid of theirs. The danger of not doing that is that they grow up with a pseudo-personality and fall victim to other narcissists and end up being trapped in a violent relationship themselves as adults.

Chapter 2

Recognizing that you are Living with a narcissist

The consequences of being married to a narcissistic guy can be intense. To begin with, it is difficult in itself to figure out if you are married to a narcissist or not.

Here are 20 telltale signs that you are married to a narcissist to help you navigate your narcissistic marital issues and understand narcissistic abuse.

1. Grand self-esteem

One of the most obvious and conspicuous symptoms of a narcissistic husband or wife is that your companion has exaggerated self-esteem.

They see themselves as flawless and extraordinary.

They also believe that this is how their family, friends, colleagues, and acquaintances also see them because this is what they desire to portray.

2. Lack of sensitivity

Another evident indication that you have a narcissistic partner is their total lack of sensitivity.

Empathy is a person's capability to recognize another person's emotions and thoughts. You can be intuitive and not be in love with an individual.

But when it's the other way around, it's not the same.. You cannot be in love or communicate affection when you do not have sensitivity.

Remember: Love is impossible without empathy, for it is empathy that differentiates emotions of infatuations from actual love.

Lack of sensitivity may be hard to see, but, it is demonstrated in behaviors such as speaking cruel things to you without them blinking an eye.

If you are married to a narcissist, they won't demonstrate any concern towards you or anybody around them (although they can be good at pretending).

3. Loves himself

There is nothing a narcissist value more than himself. They adore speaking about themselves and the things they like. They always attempt to shift the conversation around themselves.

4. Exhibit manipulative and self-serving behaviors

While it may be unkind to say, a narcissist will only marry someone if they can benefit from the union or the partner.

If you have a narcissistic partner and you asked them, "do you love me because you need me, or do you need me because you love me?"

If they were honest, they would inform you that they adore you because they need you.

But of course, they won't say that because they know that is not what you need to hear, and to keep you they will tell you what you want to hear. They implement different psychological techniques to influence you.

If you're pondering if you are married to a narcissist, it's well worth watching out for manipulative and self-serving behaviors. An illustration of this is guilt-tripping or unfavorable comparison.

Using the force of words, they could probably inform you, "Aren't you grateful that I married you?" (guilt trip) Or "You're so terrible at cookery! My partner was greater than you" (negative comparison).

If you've heard any of these expressions, or comparable in your relationship, you might be married to a narcissist.

Take us 'am I married to a narcissist quiz' to know if you are indeed married to a narcissist.

5. Show off

Another one of the 'narcissistic husband traits' or indication of a narcissistic partner is their need to enhance their ego by identifying themselves with important or powerful people and boasting about their affiliation with them.

6. Charming and polished

At the beginning of your relationship, you can't help but gaze at your now husband or wife. When they arrived at the room, they would brighten it up, and you weren't the only one to observe, but everyone did!

Your then companion would have been attractive and sophisticated. Even flawless! A little too flawless, perhaps?

Another evident indication that you're married to a narcissist is that they're just too attractive (or they were at the beginning – when they were wooing you).

By evaluating the charisma element, you can find out if you are married to an egotistical partner. Have they stopped beguiling you now they've captured you?

But do you see them beguiling other people and question what changed, or even flinch at the fakeness you observe having become used to your partner's characteristics? These are typical indications that you are married to a narcissist.

7. Adores beautiful objects

Nothing but the finest. A narcissistic partner would partake in purchasing expensive clothes and accouterments to project an opulent demeanor. Especially someone who does not have any extraordinary collection of abilities.

8. Bad conversationalists

A conversation is excellent when there is a pleasant movement, and an interchange of thoughts and opinions exchanged between two or more individuals.

It becomes a poor conversation when someone interrupts another person and interjects their own stories as if the other people in the group do not exist.

We've all encountered this type of conversation, but did you realize that this is a symptom of a narcissistic personality disorder?

Of course, it's not always the case if you are with somebody who is brimming with enthusiasm over something or anxious and concerned about a situation they may be too preoccupied with that situation to attend to you, but the pattern will be transient.

The interruption pattern with a narcissist will be continuous.

When you're married to a narcissist, anticipate conversations to lose fluidity because your narcissistic partner will place the attention back towards them, particularly if you're diverting from providing them attention.

Having an involved social media existence does not necessarily indicate that a person might be a narcissist, but this characteristic of a narcissistic partner is another component in the jigsaw.

10. Embellish anecdotes and accomplishments

Another characteristic of a narcissistic husband or wife is how they share their experiences and achievement with (or to in a narcissist's case) others.

Don't get me wrong; there is nothing wrong with having a feeling of accomplishment, but, to a narcissist, these stories and accomplishments are so exaggerated that they can seem preposterous.

The amplification of stories and accomplishments is a manipulative strategy used by narcissists to get people to like them.

On a more dangerous level, they could use you to deceive you into believing you have fraudulent recollections, which is called 'gaslighting.'

11. His requirements are above others

Marriage is many times a compromise wherein you place your partner's wants above yours as a means to demonstrate your love and dedication to them.

However, everything in the life of a narcissist revolves around his wants. They are satisfied as long as their requirements are being fulfilled. Even if that means you have to endure or not be satisfied with your existence.

12. No consideration for personal boundaries

A marriage has standards, and these rules make it possible for two individuals to be free (sounds a bit sarcastic), but when you think about it, it's accurate.

There are no rules when you are married to a narcissist because they will use your love for them as a justification to disregard whatever limitations you may have placed on them since they are, after all, "above" it.

Having no consideration for your boundaries is another indication that you are married to a narcissist.

13. No give and take

Given that a narcissist overlooks the most general principle of 'compromise' in a marriage, they would even lack the sensitivity to address your obligations.

They expect to constantly be the center of attention in your relationship, and there is no room for compromise.

14. Fluctuating disposition

Do you feel tugged in and driven away by your partner frequently? If you responded 'yes,' you might be married to a narcissist.

The hot and cool behavior is a way to manipulate you into their self-serving methods.

Your companion may love-bomb you today, and tomorrow, they won't even take up their phone when you contact them.

If you observe this or similar patterns, your companion is submitting you to inconsistent reinforcement, which makes you just like, want, and adore them even more.

15. Behaves like a juvenile

As we grow mature and become more conscious of our circumstances, we learn to control ourselves. This characteristic is witnessed, particularly when we do not get what we desire.

For a narcissist, however, everything is personal. They would go to extremes, create outbursts, act out, or make a commotion if they do not get what they want or if in case you disagree with them.

16. Can't conceal for long

Marriage is such an extensive commitment that even the most cunning egocentric won't be able to conceal their real nature.

If your marriage displays any narcissistic relationship characteristics, in time, they will become very transparent. So, it is acceptable to take your time and not be judgmental of your partner too quickly.

Give them time, and ultimately, you will know if they are whom you imagined them to be.

17. Superiority compound

Not positive how to tell if you are married to a narcissist? Well, do they believe that they are superior to everyone else?

If yes, then you could be married to a narcissist.

They significantly associate themselves with someone who has better intelligence than others around them.

Even though they might actually be endowed with a lot of knowledge, they would detest it when people do not consider them as someone superior.

18. Can't tolerate criticism

Given that a narcissist has an inflated ego, their ability to tolerate criticism would be little to none. Any type of criticism would not be accepted by him, and if someone challenges him, it might even make him extremely furious.

19. Never accepts accountability

For a megalomaniac 'it is never his fault'. Don't expect your narcissistic partner to accept accountability for their actions.

Be it a problem at work, with an acquaintance, or even at home, they would go to excessive measures to not acknowledge and own up to their blunders.

20. Control maniac

Calling your partner 'controlling' during a disagreement is something that many of has done; even if it isn't accurate, we do not always recognize that during our confrontations.

However, for a narcissistic husband or a narcissistic wife, this word becomes very true very quickly. The domineering character of a narcissistic partner can even contribute to a domestically violent relationship.

Chapter 3

Dealing with A Narcissist Husband

You are most definitely here to find out how to survive with an egotistical partner. But is it even feasible or beneficial for you? That's a legitimate question and one this article takes care of as well.

Honestly, we are all a little egotistical by nature. After all, we are people. But conquering this propensity is a must if you are to live a satisfying existence. A characteristic of real affection is placing the requirements of another before yours, at least for the most part. Narcissism contradicts that.

Ever heard of Narcissus? He is a character in Greek mythology who was renowned for his attractiveness. The narrative goes that he fell in love with his projection rather than exploring personal relationships. Guess what? His character is the genesis of the word "narcissist," which means "an unhealthy obsession with oneself."

So, should you call it quits and depart if your partner is a narcissist? After all, you deserve better, right? However, you shouldn't rush the trigger just yet, particularly if you adore your partner. Here's why:

Your partner isn't being intentionally unkind; he is unwell. Yes, that's correct! A narcissistic personality disorder is a physical condition. This means with the proper information, you can discover a sustainable solution. All hope isn't gone.

So, hold in there. Help has arrived on how you should cope with an egotistical partner. To start you off, here are the indications that you are dealing with an egotistical partner.

Is Your Husband A Narcissist?

Before proceeding any further, you have to be completely positive your partner is a narcissist. After all, he wasn't like that when you met, right?

This is a perplexing problem to contend with. However, with the proper information, you can approach it head-on without second-guessing yourself. Here are the primary indicators that you are dealing with a partner who is a narcissist.

Gaslighting

Being gaslighted is a traumatizing experience. It's a circumstance where your partner makes you question your rationality.

For example, you challenge him on an issue, and before you realize it, he has flipped the tables on you. Suddenly, it's your responsibility.

Why can't you be understanding? Are you positive you aren't becoming your mother? This is why your previous relationships didn't amount to much.

Narcissists adore this strategy; why? It transfers the responsibility from them. Not only that but by also bringing you down psychologically, they become 'better' than you.

It's disgusting behavior, honestly.

Negative Criticism

It is impossible to be comfortable with everything your partner does. It's completely reasonable to disagree on topics in marriage. But if your partner is prone to negative criticism, then you have a significant problem.

Couples in successful relationships speak things out; it's the mature method of settling difficulties. But you can't come to an understanding if your partner is egotistical and constantly ridicules your efforts, tears you down, or just straight-up attacks you.

A narcissistic partner does this to enhance his vanity or escape accountability. This is disheartening because you might finish up believing you are insufficient.

A 'Grey' Marriage

Do you remember what courtship was like? The concentrated concentration he gave you? His intricate displays of dedication? His unending declarations of everlasting love? Those were the happy times.

This is presumably why you fell for him. It hurts but narcissists know that as women, we are enthusiasts of romanticism and charisma.

When it benefits him, such an individual will make you believe you are the only thing he cares about. However, once you are married, the façade dissolves. The colorful courtship is replaced by a drab, boring, and melancholy marriage where passion and hilarity are in short supply.

There is a rationale for this. Like players, a narcissist views every woman as a conquest. He will go to great efforts to get you with the solitary objective of expanding their ego. Once the 'conquest' stops, he makes you his emotional pounding bag.

Serenades become attacks, and instead of making you giggle, he ridicules you. A complete 180 change of events that makes you question your rationality.

He Intentionally Makes You Jealous

No self-respecting guy goes out of his way to make a woman feel terrible about herself. It's just simply incorrect.

But try conveying this to an egotistical partner. It's a method of making you seek his blessing on every problem. It's screwed up, but it works. Think about it. If someone you adore compares you to other women or frequently flirts around, wouldn't it make you feel inadequate?

As a consequence, you might go out of your way to try and satisfy his preposterous expectations. In a twisted manner, he gets to bolster his vulnerable self-esteem and dominate you in one falling stroke.

I know, it's frigid and completely Machiavellian.

He Is Incredibly Jealous

Oh! The delicious absurdity.

A self-obsessed partner is all right about making you envious but he bursts a spark when your attention moves to someone else. Don't give it out if you can't take it is a strange concept to narcissists.

It always has to be about him; your business, colleagues, and family can take a vacation. God forbid that another male shows you attention, even if it's innocuous.

Yes, males are territorial by temperament. But would a steady partner be envious of your child? Of course not! But studies indicate that narcissistic partners respond unpredictably after you give birth.

Now, it can swing both ways. He will either despise the fact that you have to concentrate on the neonate, or he will disregard you completely and focus exclusively on the child. Either way, it's not a wholesome condition.

Lack of Empathy

A narcissist will always place himself first in every circumstance.

As you know, this transforms matrimony into a terrible experience. A relationship is a two-way highway with give and take. If your partner disregards your emotions and doesn't view you as an equal, then what's the point? You can't depend on him, he won't support you in any significant manner, and he will only pitch in when it benefits him.

Without understanding, your marriage is as good as gone. The trouble is, a self-obsessed partner will place the responsibility on you when you bring up the matter. He will assert you are hard to please, disrespectful, and prone to complaining.

That said, how do you cope with an egotistical husband? You will next learn about that.

How to Live with A Narcissist Husband

Living with a megalomaniac is by no means a vacation. While calling it quits and abandoning the ship might seem like a good idea, there are tried and proven methods of dealing with a narcissist. Read on to find out more.

Don't Be Baited

A common characteristic with all narcissists is that they adore attention; they will do anything and everything to get you to concentrate on them. Understanding this is essential. It enables you to see the attention-seeking behaviors for what they are.

Make no mistake, this won't be a cakewalk. Remember, narcissists, are expert manipulators. Since your partner knows you well, he will know which triggers to press.

You have to keep your head on a swivel when you are interacting with him. Watch what he says and contemplate before responding. It's exhausting, but this way, you won't readily fall for his methods. This pertains to both favorable and detrimental practices. Don't presume anything.

By meeting preposterous behavior with coolness and equanimity, he is denied the gratification of drawing a response from you. That's perfectly how to manage a narcissistic partner without confrontation.

Set Up Boundaries

Setting up boundaries in a coupling might seem excessive. But difficult circumstances call for extraordinary measures. Don't let a narcissistic partner have his way every time. Set a boundary in the ground and let him know when he crosses it.

The trouble with a self-absorbed partner is when you give him an inch, he will take a mile. You have to foot down on topics that make you uncomfortable.

Now, there is a high possibility that he will initiate a disagreement if you adopt this strategy. But remember, don't accept his lure. It's what he anticipates.

Call him out on his behaviors with determination. Don't hesitate when he stages an outburst. That's how to cope with an egotistical partner hell-bent on denying you independence.

After all, what else can he do? Sulk? Insult you? Ignore you? Unless you accept it, these methods do not influence you. Setting up boundaries tells him you mean business, and that you will not be shoved around.

Of course, this won't happen immediately. It requires patience, determination, and fortitude.

Stand Up for Yourself

Despite what your experience living with a narcissist has made you believe, you have a strong will.

It might be suppressed as a consequence of a dysfunctional marriage, but make no mistake, it is deep within you. Nurturing it back to life is the only way you can withstand a narcissistic partner. So, how can you do this?

By sticking up for yourself.

As I said earlier, speak out to your partner when he does something you don't concur with. Of course, he will use every tactic in his book to turn the tables on you but don't back down.

A piece of advice: Though it takes time, you have to suppress your wrath in such circumstances. Yes, you have every right to be ticked off. But, giving in to your anger is playing directly into his hands.

While wrath is a powerful feeling, it's ineffective against a self-absorbed partner. Instead, face him head-on with clear and reasonable thought.

Think about it. How would you manage an unreasonable child? By screaming at them, therefore reducing yourself to their level, or by choosing the high road?

Dealing with an egotistical partner shouldn't be any different.

This won't be simple by any means. But, before you can walk, you must first slither. It's all about consistency. Chip away at the situation bit by bit. Re-learning how to adore someone, particularly a partner with narcissistic inclinations, is an exhausting process.

In time, you will be able to stare him down without flinching. You will break down his nonsensical and egotistical requests with calm and reasonable counterarguments.

He will come to understand that you are not his emotional plaything but a self-aware woman who won't take his foolishness laying down. Now, how to manage an egotistical partner like an expert.

Do Not Make Excuses for Him

Even though you adore your partner, making allowances for his harmful behavior isn't beneficial. Yes, narcissism is a condition, but this doesn't justify the negative ways in which he regards you.

He knows better.

Otherwise, he wouldn't have troubled with courting you before sealing the marriage. Despite what he tells you, your self-obsessed partner is frightened at the possibility of losing you.

His egotistical behavior is intended to make you believe that you need him more. In actuality, it is the opposite way around.

Let me let you in on a secret: Narcissists have delicate personalities. It's why they need continuous reinforcement and adulation. This demonstrates one thing: You are still in control.

But, creating allowances for your partner means you will end up condemning yourself for his behavior. Of course, this is what a narcissist wants: someone else assuming the accountability for their disaster.

If you resolve to make your marriage work, then you will have to see your partner for what he is.

This is the cornerstone of managing an egotistical partner. Otherwise, your self-esteem will be shattered in the process of your matrimony.

Go Back To 'Doing Your Thing'

Narcissists want what they cannot have.

Remember what you were like before yearning for your husband? You had an existence of your own.

From ambitions and aspirations to objectives that kept you motivated. You presumably stayed in contact with your family and your network of acquaintances. You had interests of your own and thoughts that kept you up at night.

So, what changed?

You became secluded, and all you could think about was making your partner passionately in love with you. But there is only one problem: No matter how much effort you offer, it's never enough.

It is conceivable that over time, you separated yourself from your acquaintances and relatives. You gave up your interests and your objectives and took a second position. But don't tear yourself up.

Despite how you might feel, it isn't your responsibility and the injury isn't irreversible. Rebuilding your life and cleaning up old relationships will get your thoughts off your dysfunctional marriage. Of course, your partner won't embrace this transformation.

After all, he requires you to be secluded and dependent on him. Reigniting your feeling of individuality will work marvels for your emotional well-being. Don't be hesitant to request assistance. You don't have to aspire to do this by yourself, and you don't have to.

Friends and family will serve as a support structure in your hardest moments. Spending time with them will remember you what it's like to be the center of attention for a change. Be determined, don't vacillate in your direction.

You had an existence before your marriage, and you can still restore it regardless of your present circumstances.

While this procedure will take time, the outcome will be worth it.

The greatest part? It's a win-win circumstance for you.

Your partner can either come along on your conditions or be consigned to the pavement. His decision.

Frequently Asked Questions

Is Narcissism A Personality Disorder?

Yes, it is. Otherwise referred to as NPD, it is mentioned with other psychiatric illnesses. Examples include schizoid personality disorder, borderline personality disorder, obsessive-compulsive disorder, and others. The best method to approach narcissistic personality conditions is by getting medical counsel.

Now, your partner might not be receptive to the notion. However, you might get through to him by describing how his behavior is destroying your marriage.

A mental health practitioner will provide a prognosis and provide sustainable solutions to the problem. But there is a caveat.

Narcissists are expert manipulators and falsehoods. Unless he desires assistance, your partner will attempt to deceive the doctor. And the unfortunate thing is, there is a good possibility he will achieve.

Can A Narcissist Person Become Physically Abusive?

It's a coin flip.

It depends on your husband's predisposition to aggression and his personality. However, it could happen to you, particularly if you don't take a position early on in your marriage.

Remember, a narcissist will steadily press your boundaries attempting to figure out how much you can handle. This is why it is essential to speak up for yourself.

Do not make the mistake of condoning violent behavior. Being self-obsessed is one thing; cruelty is a whole other ball game. Call him out for it and inform your loved one the instant it happens. It will keep him in control.

A piece of wisdom. There is no purpose in remaining in a violent situation. You are better off strolling away instead. Trust me, nothing is worth that degree of disrespect.

Can A Narcissist Husband Change?

In all honesty, it depends on his disposition and the importance he places on your relationship. Remember, most narcissists do not recognize they have a problem.

If your partner doesn't want to lose you, then he will take the necessary measures to be a stronger guy. It will be challenging but he will transform for the better over time.

However, if your partner is inebriated by his exaggerated ego, then nothing can be done. You will have to determine whether to depart or remain. It all depends on you. Choose carefully.

All that said, now the game is in your court. Armed with all this information, you will be in a perfect situation to make the right decision on how to deal with an egotistical partner.

Chapter 4

Things Narcissist Hate

You undoubtedly spend a great deal of time feeling dejected and frustrated by the narcissist in your life. You see how they abuse other people (and yourself), and it's disgusting.

You know what you don't like in your relationship. But have you ever pondered how to make a megalomaniac miserable?

To be clear, striving to make a narcissist uncomfortable has its place for a short time, but I don't advocate focusing on it for too long since it will surely have an influence on your mental health and energy levels.

But, if you need a rapid remedy, let's get into the top 12 things all narcissists detest.

How to Make a Narcissist Miserable

1 - Lack of Acknowledgment

It's no secret that most narcissists delight in admiration and affirmation (except for 'closet narcissists'). They depend on continuous approbation to preserve their sense of fundamental value. To accomplish this objective, they consume (or pilfer) the energy of other people to feel good about themselves.

Do you ever ponder why narcissists don't seem to mind the unfavorable attention? It's because unfavorable recognition also feeds their narcissistic flames. The negativity is still attention, and any type of attention gives them the motivation to keep trying. It motivates them to keep demonstrating themselves.

In fact, they often like negative attention better because if you're still troubled by their relationship offenses, they can leverage this to strengthen the trauma bond and keep you attached and intertwined!

Therefore, a dearth of acknowledgment is a genuine danger. To a narcissist, indifference is even more of a problem than animosity. They'd rather you have an unfavorable opinion than have no opinion at all.

Narcissists can't abide when no one is giving attention to them. They don't know how to feel significant or exceptional if they aren't the center of the universe or devouring someone's thoughts. This is also why the conventional Grey Rock approach is often fruitless and why complete abstinence is the best option (or extremely modified contact if you share children with them).

2 – When People Speak Factually

Have you ever given careful attention to how a megalomaniac speaks? They use extravagant, long-winded language saturated with the exaggerated sentiment. They distort reality to suit their viewpoint, and they believe their truth is always the truth.

Additionally, through the use of cognitive empathy, they've spent their entire lifetimes witnessing the emotional language of other people and using it to their advantage. So, when you communicate in facts instead of using feeling, they instinctively comprehend they have less of an upper edge.

Therefore, they detest when someone challenges them with evidence instead of feeling it. They will typically counterattack with more arguments or hysteria. This immature reaction simply indicates that they feel out of control. They attempt to heighten the conversation's intensity by launching an emotional temper outburst.

If anything, this relationship only emphasizes the narcissist's irresponsibility. Their incapacity to assimilate facts demonstrates their incompetence in approaching most grownup relationships. They are not proficient in the language of facts because they are always lying and concealing things, so speaking throws them off-balance.

3 – Authority

Narcissists despise authority. That's because they detest having to account for anybody but themselves. Any feeling of authority challenges their intrinsic demands for power and control.

It's not uncommon for narcissists to have problems at employment, education, or with the police. Has the psychopath in your life had numerous jobs? Are they frequently getting disciplined for their behavior?

While narcissists can be intellectual, they often come across as aggressive and unsuitable in professional environments. If challenged by their inappropriate behavior, they prefer to reject or rationalize their role.

Of course, it's no surprise that most authoritative figures despise dealing with narcissists. Supervisors find them disorderly and unreasonable. They can't comprehend why the individual can't follow fundamental instructions without such explosive responses.

4 – Being Told No

Of all things a narcissist dislikes, being told no (and following through with it) leads the list. Narcissists are accustomed to manipulating and weaseling their way to their desired outcome.

Often, they'll draw all the breaks to accomplish this goal. They've spent their whole careers persuading individuals to satisfy their requirements. They never pause to think about how their emotions influence the situation.

That's why telling them no- and being uncompromising on your stance- often causes such a furious response. A narcissist isn't just angry about the denial- they're genuinely perplexed by it!

Narcissists can't honestly comprehend why someone would reject them. Because they lack genuine sensitivity, they can't comprehend what must be going on in your thoughts. Moreover, even if they attempt to understand it, they refuse to embrace this reality.

5 – Implementing Consequences

Have you ever attempted to establish a boundary with a narcissist? How well did it go? Most likely, you attempted to establish a restriction, and they responded in one of three ways:

Dismissing you completely and gaslighting your emotions

Acknowledging their blunder, resolving to change, and then doing nothing to change

Reacting with extreme anger, threats, or even physical violence

Narcissists can't tolerate any serious repercussions. They can't see when they're wrong, and they can't comprehend how someone would ever believe they're wrong. Even if the narcissist was aware of this, they would just disregard it.

As a result, they tend to respond disproportionately to boundaries and serious conversations as a means to intimidate you and drive you into submission.

Unfortunately, many people simply give up on attempting to institute repercussions with narcissists. Because they want to prevent a potential confrontation, they capitulate and disregard their emotions. How many times have you averted putting a genuine boundary because that's just how they are?

6 - Losing at Anything

Have you ever witnessed small toddlers playing a board game? If so, you undoubtedly witnessed plenty of deceptive behaviors and theatrical responses to losing. It's permissible when the participants are three years old, but what happens when you're referring to full-fledged adults?

Narcissists can approach children, in that they tend to be exceedingly bitter losers. They struggle to accept defeat, and they also tend to strike out when it happens. A few situations may occur:

They constantly proclaim the individual in control (boss/referee) was incompetent

They endeavor to slander or humiliate the victor

They pretend they didn't care about victory

They demand that they "let the other person" assume the limelight

They refuse to acknowledge that they lost and uncomfortably behave as if they're the actual victor (you may have experienced this by hearing after you've left them, that they've informed everyone they're the one who left you!)

7 – Public Humiliation

Because they are bitter losers, narcissists can't manage actual or perceived public embarrassment. They just can't tolerate the possibility of failure. To them, public degradation is the ultimate expression of failure.

We all know that narcissists have exceedingly delicate personalities. When they believe someone is making light of them or if they're not the recognized expert or authority in a public situation, it jolts their existence.

As a consequence, they'll do anything to safeguard their vulnerable psyche. Some typical reactions include:

Making aggressive or emotionally-charged threats

Trying to outdo the audience by turning on them

Screaming or shouting

Walking away with evident wrath

Laughing it off in public only to strike out later on loved ones later

Making up falsehoods about anyone who is a genuine authority

8 – Expectations of Commitment

Most narcissists are horrible with commitment. Although they believe they receive all feelings of devotion, they don't typically provide it themselves. As a consequence, when they get into relationships, they don't consider other people's requirements. They're only responsible for their feelings, instincts, and desires.

Unfortunately, many devoted partners cling to forlorn optimism about their narcissist transforming. They attend to how the narcissist compliments and cherishes them. They clutch onto ephemeral assurances that this time will be different.

Yet the narcissist establishes all the rules. They determine what they want to do, and they do it when they want to do it. Therefore, they can violate and modify the norms in ways that suit them.

9 - Vulnerability And Emotional Expression

Narcissists often use cognitive empathy to stimulate interest in other people's feelings. Real, empathetic understanding means placing ourselves in someone else's circumstances. We take on the emotions and experiences of the other individual.

Cognitive empathy, on the other hand, is far more pernicious and manipulative. Think about the money-hungry salesperson who preys on your uncertainty about purchasing a new vehicle.

Think about the general contractor who persuaded you that you need to replace your appliances.

Cognitive empathy means delving into someone's inner thoughts and sentiments. This strategy necessitates having an initial relationship.

Narcissists use cognitive empathy to "gain entry" into your susceptibility. They construct this feeling of confidence and camaraderie using phony benevolence and sensitivity.

At the same time, they detest vulnerability and emotional expression. They interpret it as an indication of vulnerability. Therefore, they use it to take advantage of you when your barriers are down.

10 – 99% Of Other People

Chapter 5

Narcissistic Abuse Recovery

Significant Must-Know Factors

Narcissistic abuse rehabilitation may be the most challenging thing you ever do, but if you are perusing this website you may already know that. It may seem like there is no way out of the sadness and distress that you are experiencing. Just when you believe you are gaining a handle on things, something happens and you are thrust back into uncertainty, turmoil, and conflict. It may feel like there is no way to make meaning of what occurred, or of what is still occurring, even though you may have already fled the violent relationship.

So, let's have a look at the patterns in a narcissistic relationship and what transpires afterward. This violent relationship could be a one-to-one relationship or a group circumstance, such as in a work environment or a destructive sect.

Because of the nature of psychological maltreatment, there are many variables that you have to take into consideration. Here is a summary of some of the most essential and we will evaluate each in order.

Your feelings were very controlled by the psychopath.

Your reasoning and decision-making were significantly influenced by the narcissist.

The egocentric is not going to transform.

The target of a narcissist is conditioned to be dependent on the narcissist.

Psychological violence affects individuals at many levels and it affects them very profoundly.

There were many things done to you that impacted you in ways that are outside of your consciousness.

It's not your problem.

Don't get too caught up with the word victim. Individuals dislike being labeled as victims, yet it is an accurate description of someone who has been in a relationship with a narcissist. And just because one has been a victim does not imply one will always be a victim. Individuals may and do recover from narcissistic abuse and no longer feel or act like victims.

Emotions Control

A narcissist will generally be influencing your feelings from the word go. All the adulation and compliments and making you feel good at the outset of the relationship (called love bombing) was part of the emotional control exercised by the narcissist. Being enraptured with or in love with someone, particularly when it happens quickly, indicates that the subject is not thinking very clearly or rationally.

The exhilaration or euphoria impairs one's discernment. This is why people disregard their friends and family when cautioned about the narcissist originally. They feel so wonderful that they practically have no awareness of difficulties or danger.

Later on, the narcissist learns all your vulnerable points (some of which they even invent!) and then uses these to make you feel terrible, humiliated, remorseful, frightened, undeserving, unlovable, and a whole array of other feelings.

While they have little or no feelings themselves it's fascinating just how effective they are at manipulating and influencing the emotions of those around them. And control them they do. People generally speak about having been on an emotional roller coaster during the relationship and it can even be worse after a separation.

These continuous ups and downs in the relationship keep you off balance and make it very difficult for you to think properly. It also implies that you are so occupied that you don't even have time to pause and think and ruminate on the relationship itself and what's actually going on.

Emotional manipulation generally leads to phobias, which are worries that are disproportionate to reality. Victims have anxieties about fleeing the violent relationship, believing that they may not be able to manage without the narcissist, that they may never find anyone else to adore them or that they may even perish without the narcissist. There are often intense worries about what might happen to them if they offend or disobey the narcissist or go against the narcissist in any manner.

The world the victim lives in grows narrower and narrower as time goes on, with the victim generally living in a sort of perpetual present, always watchful against disturbing the narcissist in order to escape that combustible and unpredictable temper.

As you go through your narcissistic abuse rehabilitation, beware of anyone who promises your assistance by training you to regulate your feelings.

You have had way too much control of your feelings already in the relationship and it's much more essential to be able to articulate them and to understand how they were controlled rather than to 'not feel terrible'. The issue is that as you go through a narcissistic abuse rehabilitation you are going to have poor periods for a while.

Thought management and behavior control

Influencing your feelings provides the narcissist with a very effective method to control your thoughts, your decision-making, and your behavior.

At the outset of the relationship, the narcissist makes you feel very comfortable. When you think about the narcissist, you get this lovely fuzzy feeling all over and so you make certain decisions in connection to the narcissist and you conduct in a certain manner, too. This first perception is very significant because it is often challenging for us to modify these first impressions.

Later, however, when the poor behavior comes in, it is originally pardoned and forgotten because the target has the idea that a narcissist is a wonderful person. The narcissist typically begins the violent behavior after the target has committed in some manner. It could be residing together, in business together or married, or some other degree of participation.

As the sufferer falls more and more under the influence of the narcissist the mental abuse gets more frequent and more devastating. Now, instead of advancing towards enjoyment, the sufferer begins to shift away from agony.

The narcissist causes such distress that the life of the sufferer starts to revolve around not disturbing the narcissist. The decisions the target makes and the behaviors are structured around making sure the narcissist is comfortable and has what he or she desires.

There is often an incentive and discipline structure in effect. Do something that the narcissist does not want and there is a consequence (of which there is a wide variety) and do or say what the narcissist does want and there is compensation (which are typically few and far between). An incentive can simply be that the egocentric does not initiate an argument!

The target may consider that they have the situation under control in the sense that they know how to evaluate the attitude of the narcissist and based on this they determine what they can say or do, or what they shouldn't say or do, so as not to disturb the narcissist. But this is a 'technique' of psychological torture. The narcissist has 'educated' the target on how to make such judgments by the very act of the incentive and discipline system.

Things manipulative individuals say and their consequences.

The reality that the sufferer believes they are making their own decisions has very significant repercussions. For example, it conceals from the victim the fact that the narcissist is influencing practically all of the decisions of the victim. It also means that the sufferer is encouraged to continue in the relationship because believing they are making their own decisions gives them a feeling of control.

Unfortunately, it also leads the sufferer into believing that they are accountable for various things that the narcissist accuses them of. This belief of the sufferer that they are accountable for anything terrible or wrong in the relationship is particularly difficult to unravel later on during narcissistic abuse rehabilitation.

They ain't gonna change

Victims of narcissists generally believe that the narcissist adores them and cares for them and has their best interests at heart. At least until they discover that the narcissist is heartless and even then, it takes a while to get your mind around the notion that some people don't have feelings. Until this is completely acknowledged there is always optimism that the narcissist might transform and the sufferer continues to desire a relationship that is equitable or where they are handled kindly.

The recollections of the pleasant moments at the outset of the relationship strengthen these aspirations. Sometimes the victim believes that they might be mistaken about the narcissist and that they (the victim) deserve the poor behavior for the way they are and this causes the victim to think that if only they could change the narcissist would be better.

Added to these things are the assurances of the narcissist that he or she will transform and this also plays on the feelings of the sufferer and provides hope.

All these activities are part of psychological torture and mind control. The egocentric is not going to transform.

If you believed that you were superior to everyone around you and that you deserved the finest of everything and all your troubles were because of the idiots and incompetents around you, would you sense a need to change? Of course not. This is why narcissists rarely go for treatment for their narcissism.

Watch out, though, if they offer to go to counseling with you as a means to get you back. They still ain't gonna change. They will, however, discover more about what's going on in your mind and that information will be used against you.

It's also a genuine catastrophe if they deceive the counselor and contrive to place all the responsibility on you. This is so devastating that if you believe you are in a relationship with a narcissist (or a psychopath) you should never go to couples counseling with them.

Because they don't change, the more time you are with them the more opportunity they have to manipulate you. This is why all the specialists recommend no communication. The sooner you get away from them the simpler and speedier your narcissistic abuse rehabilitation will be. Maintaining communication with them, whether in person or by email or messages, means they continue to perform mental games with you and you fail. It is as straightforward as that.

But... getting away from them is not a simple affair at all. They have committed a lot of time and energy to mold you to be the way they want you to be so they generally won't give you up without a struggle.

In the same way that in business they say that it's easier to keep a customer than get a customer, for the narcissist, it's simpler to retain a target than to go through all the effort to generate a new one.

You can expect them to apologize, tell you that they made a mistake, tell you that you made a mistake, tell you that you will never find anyone to love you like they do (thank goodness!), threaten you, threaten suicide, promise you the sun, moon, and stars, and a variety of other emotional manipulation techniques. Then they frequently go through them all again!

But there is something else that is very compelling that pulls you back to them.

The Interdependence

An essential element of psychological abuse and mental control is interdependence. There are things that a narcissist does and says that create attachment in their victims.

This is irrespective of the disposition of the sufferer before the relationship. It does NOT imply that a sufferer has a dependent disposition, is co-dependent, or has substance difficulties. Most specialists in the field of mind control concur that anyone is susceptible to being ensnared by a narcissist. This implies that there is no particular personality type that is susceptible to being captivated by a narcissist or psychopath. Everybody is susceptible. Even psychiatrists who deal with narcissists and psychopaths may go into an encounter with one of them, knowing they are a narcissist, and still be deceived!

So how particularly do they establish the dependency? One method is juxtaposing critiques with compliments. The sufferer feels good with the commendation and terrible with the condemnation.

This builds up in the sufferer a yearning for approbation from the provocateur. When they are reprimanded by the manipulator, whom they hold in high esteem, they feel that they have let the manipulator down and it often encourages them to work harder for the manipulator so that they receive a commendation later instead of criticism.

Eventually, their well-being depends on the attitude of the manipulator and whether the manipulator is speaking positive or negative things to them. In extreme instances, the sufferer even depends on the narcissist to know who they are, too.

Narcissists also undermine the self-confidence of the sufferers and cause them to question themselves. When a victim has their ideas and opinions ridiculed and belittled and they are made to feel terrible and foolish for thinking differently from the narcissist, ultimately the victim learns to question themselves. And if they question themselves, who do they look to know what to believe and do? To the egotistical, of course. By doing this they believe it will help them not to get into problems. If the psychopath instructs them what to do, there should be no difficulty.

Of course, it never works out this way because the unpredictable character of the narcissist means that there is always conflict. After all, nothing is ever enough for the megalomaniac!

This interdependence pushes the sufferer back to the narcissist all the time. The indoctrination of the narcissist is like master software that the target employs to reason and make decisions. If the target has any inquiries or concerns, they ask themselves, 'what would the provocateur say or do, or what would they want me to say or do?' And this is how the sufferer organizes their existence. In essence, you could say that the narcissist becomes their mission in life.

Now it is becoming more apparent just how widespread the influence of the narcissist is.

The Personality

I said that narcissist affects their subject at many levels. He (or she) influences the surroundings that the sufferer inhabits. He influences their behavior. He impacts their capabilities. He also influences the beliefs of the victim (and some of the victim's beliefs that were implanted by the narcissist can be even stronger than typical, healthy beliefs). And eventually, the narcissist affects the personality of the sufferer.

A person's personality is generally consistent over time, and when we know something about a person's personality, we feel we know how a person will act in certain situations, allowing us to trust that person. If we believe that a person's personality is their fundamental nature and is composed of their patterns of thoughts, feelings, and behaviors as well as the psychological processes that underlie them, then a person's personality tends to remain fairly consr time.

Now what the narcissist does is essentially 'unfreeze' the personality, adjustments are made and this new but deceptive personality is sealed in place. When friends and family state to the sufferer that they have altered in their relationship with a narcissist, they are referencing the outcome of this process.

Outsiders may state that they don't recognize the person anymore, this person may have been extroverted, confident, cheerful, powerful, sociable, easygoing, and full of life.

Since the relationship started the person has become, introverted, concerned, melancholy, clandestine, lacking humor, reclusive, frightened, and dependent on the partner, they have lost their brightness, and they seem despondent almost. The strangers often observe they hardly recognize their companion anymore.

How does the narcissist do this? Well, all the condemnation, degradation, ridiculing, screaming, name-calling, and derogatory things has the effect of making the individual feel terrible about themselves. The sufferer ends up believing that who they are is the source of the difficulties they have. This is also what sects do to followers, by the way. They magnify the problems that members have, then connect these to the person's manner of being in the world.

This encourages the individual to improve themselves in some manner. And in what manner is that? In whatever manner the megalomaniac suggests, of course.

The narcissist has all the solutions, they know what's best, their thoughts and ideas are flawless and if only everyone thought as they did, everyone could have an existence as ideal as theirs.

So the target is pushed along a road where they have to believe what the narcissist wants, think the way the narcissist wants, and behave the way the narcissist wants.

In this manner the narcissist shapes the personality of the person to be the way they want it, that is, subservient, doing the bidding of the narcissist, believing every word the narcissist says, making the narcissist's wants and needs a priority, and providing all time and attention to the narcissist.

In this manner, the victim ends up being dependent on the narcissist, the victim is verifying with the narcissist, in one way or another, to know what to do, to think, and to feel. (In a sick and twisted way, the narcissist then criticizes the victim for being this way, for not having their own opinions, for not being able to make decisions, and for not having any initiative.)

Anyway, this enforced personality is called the pseudo-personality and it dominates and regulates the actual personality, which is never completely obliterated. This explanation is a very helpful approach to thinking about what transpires in a narcissistic relationship.

This is not the same as a divided personality or numerous personalities. The pseudo-personality is enforced by the narcissist and it is something that is acquired. (This means that it can be unlearned.)

These two personalities help clarify many things. One illustration is the emotional struggle that occurs in the sufferer. One part of them may detest the narcissist for the way that they are handled but another part respects them and wants things to improve. One portion wishes to flee away but another can't comprehend not being in the relationship. This internal struggle between what the actual personality desires and what the pseudo-personality is conditioned to do can cause considerable suffering for the sufferer.

This may lengthen the relationship because the sufferer, unable to make sense of the situation, believes that they are the source of the problem and that the narcissist is correct about them. This is even more detrimental for the sufferer because it encourages all the erroneous notions of the narcissist.

Any narcissistic abuse rehabilitation means reversing all the conditioning of the pseudo-personality so that the person's real personality is permitted to resurface, so to speak so that it can become the guiding force and assume control once again.

Learning the intricacies

Most individuals are ignorant of how persuasion mechanisms operate. Sure, they know some fundamental concepts such as that when a business states that only a few things are remaining they are using the scarcity principle to try and make the product more attractive. Or when the commercial proclaims that 8 out of 10 cats prefer this sort of food, the information about how those 10 cats were selected is kept a secret.

But they don't comprehend that when someone flatters them, even if they know the flattery is an embellishment or just clearly not true, it still has a significant impact on them.

They may not comprehend that when a narcissist requests a favor (at the start of the relationship) that the narcissist could care less about the object they ask for, what they are verifying is their victim's reaction.

Nor do they know that when the narcissist does a favor, again they are not doing it for the advantage of the target, they are watching how the victim responds. And then later on there are numerous ways in which the narcissist 'cash in' on this favor, none of which are for the advantage of the sufferer, of course!

The victims of narcissists are not conscious of the multiplicity of things that the narcissist is doing to them behind their backs. Well, that's not precisely accurate, it doesn't even have to be behind the back of the target.

Narcissists are delighted to do things to their appearances because the narcissist knows he or she doesn't have to conceal what they are doing because the target simply doesn't know what to watch out for to safeguard themselves.

Learning about the intricacies of these things during narcissistic abuse rehabilitation is crucial if a victim does not want to be ensnared again by the next narcissist they encounter.

All these secret things...

Let's suppose you are playing cards with someone and of the 52 cards you have 5, they have 42 and there are 5 cards face down on the table. Your cards are face up on the table in front of you and visible to the other person. They are clutching their 42 cards in their palms and close to their torso so that you cannot see them. You don't know what the objective of the game is so you don't know what you have to do to succeed. Nor do you know what the rules are and the other individual can modify the rules at any moment.

This is what it's like to be a companion of a narcissistic individual.

Are you going to win? The chances are very much weighted against you.

If you lose, is it your responsibility that you lost? Absolutely not.

If you don't have information about the system, if essential things are intentionally concealed from you, then you cannot, by definition, be making educated judgments.

If a patient is not advised that a substantial, acknowledged danger of his operation is blindness, for example, then when he signs the permission form he cannot be considered to have provided informed consent. If an investor is not informed that the business is losing money but is made to believe that the company is doing well, if he invests then he has been deceived.

In the same manner, you were misled into the relationship with the psychopath. You were made to believe that the narcissist was knowledgeable, compassionate, affectionate, thoughtful, and a generally pleasant person. You were deceived. Important information was intentionally withheld from you until well into the relationship.

You have marketed one thing, you were handed something completely different. You thought you were receiving a healthy, caring relationship, instead, you were handed a pseudo-personality and your time, energy, money, privacy, creativity, and health were stolen away from you.

It's not your problem

You are not accountable for actions that you did not realize were occurring. You can't be faulted for these situations and it's essential that you don't criticize yourself.

The essential point to understand here is that the pseudo-personality is conditioned to assume accountability for anything negative or for anything that goes wrong. The narcissist makes himself out to be blameless and focuses the responsibility at those around him. You were typically first in the shooting line. There is so much guilt sent your way that ultimately you believe it and embrace it. This is a very profoundly entrenched tendency in victims of narcissistic abuse and takes a while to get free of.

There are many tactics the narcissist employs to establish this perception. For example, the narcissist will often do something to intentionally antagonize you. Then you respond as any typical healthy individual would in such a circumstance.

Let's suppose you get enraged and respond. The narcissist then asserts that you are argumentative and confrontational. This aggravates you more and you respond again.

The narcissist then points out that he was correct because you are still furious and fighting back. At that moment, it often seems that the narcissist is correct, you are furious and you are fighting, and so you may contemplate stepping down because you believe that it may be your fault.

But the wrinkle here is that the narcissist initiated the circumstance. He or she put it up. He was sufficiently aggravating or disrespectful about it that it would have been almost impossible not to be agitated about it. Your reaction was a natural and typical response to the circumstance. This is one essential point to understand about this circumstance.

The second essential point in this scenario is that you were experiencing wrath and responding. These are practices. This does not imply that you are particularly confrontational or argumentative. This is another variation that the narcissist introduces. He takes a behavior and uses it to disparage you at the level of personality.

Between criticizing someone for what they do and condemning them for who they are, there is a huge difference. The latter is much more damaging and much more detrimental. In reality, it's one of the ways that the narcissist undermines your individuality as described above.

Narcissistic abuse recovery is challenging

I have enumerated many concepts here and as you can begin to see, there are loads of things to consider and many things that need to be understood to go through a narcissistic abuse rehabilitation process and come out of it free of the narcissist and free of the influence of the narcissist.

It is a process of education where you learn about narcissists, their motivations, their actions, and how they think as well as the complexities of influence processes and detrimental mind control. It's not enough to just keep thinking over things in your mind or to just keep writing about your experiences.

It's important to have fresh information to make sense of what was done to you and to be able to 'set things in their position'. Without new information and a new way of thinking about your situation, you just end up going in circles in your mind, and while over time you may feel 'not as terrible' about things, the narcissist continues to interfere in your thinking and your decision-making.

Working with a professional in this field is the best thing you can do because they will help you to avoid mistakes, they will speed up your narcissistic abuse rehabilitation and they will help you to surmount problem ideas and beliefs that you didn't even realize were affecting you.

Conclusion

Learning how to live with a narcissistic partner means coming to terms with distressing behavior, such as frequent put-downs, entitlement, lack of sensitivity, and manipulation. You can use techniques to make life simpler, such as exercising self-care, establishing healthy boundaries, and remembering that you aren't to fault for any of these narcissistic partner characteristics.

Ultimately, your companion will likely need to pursue psychotherapy to make any permanent adjustments to his behavior. If your relationship is struggling due to selfishness, and other techniques have not worked, you might have to demand that your companion goes to psychotherapy with you. You may even go so far as to offer him an ultimatum.

At the end of the day, nobody should have to put up with harassment. It may be time to plan an escape and seek assistance if living with a narcissistic spouse is having a negative impact on your physical or mental health or if aggressive acts put your safety in jeopardy.

84480584R10056